Live Slowly

_____

More Life, More Joy,
More Purpose

Damon Janis
www.LiveSlowly.com

Contents

Why Read this Book?

When will you slow down and fully live?

You know when it's time to make changes in your life. That's why you're reading this book: it's time.

For many this happens after a major tragedy that requires us to create a new life.

And that's what happened to me.

Tiffany, my cherished wife of 27 years, my teen sweetheart, my best friend and lover, died from stage IV colon cancer at the age of 47.

Some of you reading this book have had an awful awakening event in your life.

The loss of a loved one such as I experienced, a financial setback that results in debilitating financial stress and an uncertain future, money troubles, a child who's become an addict and is destroying their life and yours, an unfaithful spouse. The list goes on.

These types of events serve as a wakeup call to life. They can become a catalyst to making changes for a better life, a happier, more joyful and meaningful life.

A life where you wake up in the morning excited for your day—instead of waking up, if you were even able to sleep, and dreading what you have to face for another day.

If you haven't had one of these events, my hope is that reading this book will motivate you to make changes in your life right now, anyway. There's no need to wait for a wake-up call.

If you have had one of these events, I hope you will find solace in these pages. I will show you that your life can improve, that you can be happy again, and that you can feel peace.

Ben Shewry, a well-known Australian chef, was forced to open his eyes to this need to change.

He explains how his desire to change came about:

We began working on this mussel dish, and a friend of mine and I had arranged to go out to where the mussel farm is. We met Lance, and Lance told me his story. He told us how when he was a young man like me, this entire industry had faced extinction. He had worked so much that he had missed a lot of his children's childhood. It really struck a chord with me. It made me realize that I was wasting a significant part of my life, and I had to change. (McGinn, 2015, 35:10)

This book is for you who are discouraged or grieving or unsettled in your life. For you who are living lives of quiet desperation. For you who feel unfulfilled and lack meaning or purpose. For you who have experienced a terrible loss. For you who struggle to get up and face each day. For you who want and need to start new.

Slowing down results in more living.

In these pages, I hope to convey the power of this idea to you. I hope to convince you that living slowly will result in more life, more joy, and more purpose.

Thank you, dear reader, for trusting me with your time and focus. I promise to do my best to use it wisely, efficiently, and helpfully.

— Damon Janis

Chapter 1

The Live Slowly Story

In 2013, my cherished wife of 26 years was diagnosed with stage IV colon cancer—that is essentially a death sentence. Statistically people don't survive this very long. She was only 46.

She lived for 17 months and died an hour after midnight on January 1, 2015. I lay in bed beside her dying body as fireworks were going off around our house celebrating the new year. It was surreal. How do you get your head and heart around the fact that the love of your life, the source of the light in your life, is actually dying?

It's impossible to convey in a couple paragraphs how devastating this was. We met at 16, instantly became best friends, and married five years later. We experienced having no money in college, finally graduating and getting our

1

feet on the ground financially, building a family and caring for, nurturing and teaching our five children.

Later in life, we were comfortable financially, but she died before we were able to enjoy the freedom that came with financial independence.

I wrote her poetry. Wrote her songs. We shared everything.

And then I was left alone to keep living while a significant part of me was no longer there. I didn't know how to put my life together again—I didn't even have the desire. It took a long time and a lot of work to come back from this devastating loss to live again.

What became a key component to success in living again was simplifying my life. I removed noise and distractions so I could focus on what counted. I made space to understand what makes me tick. In a sense, I got rid of distractions so I could find myself.

This is the essence of living slowly: minimize distractions in your life so you can find *you*. Once you know yourself, you can live intentionally to fulfill your needs and create joy.

I sold my house, gave away all of my things, and lived minimally and simply in a motorhome. I traveled around the country visiting the temples of my church and blogged about it on AllTheUSTemples.com. In these travels, I found peace and solace and quiet. There was time to think, find myself, and connect with God.

I was the Chief Technology Officer at a 100-employee company and the co-founder of a software business I started with my brother. I retired from my CTO job and worked out a deal with my brother to buy me out of our business.

I twice travelled to the remotest places in Ireland with a business mentor and friend. I sat for untold hours at lakes watching ducks. For a month, I lived on a beach and, alone, each morning watched the sunrise while the birds caught fish.

I visited and spent time with loved ones.

I brought my 18-year-old daughter home from college where she was struggling. She lived with me in the motorhome for six months and I helped her get back on her feet. Then, I brought my 28-year-old daughter, who has struggled with drug addiction, home for eight months to give her an opportunity to get on her feet, which she did for a time.

Over this time, I sought counsel from personal and business mentors to understand what I was going through and find ways to be effective in putting my life together again.

I travelled to Israel with my older brother and connected with my Jewish and religious roots.

I read books. Many books.

Books on grieving, like *A Grief Observed*.

Books on starting life again, like *Second Firsts*.

Books on creating healthy relationships, like *How to Avoid Falling in Love with a Jerk.*

Books on dealing with drug addicted children, like *Let Go Now* and *The Lost Years.*

I joined a widow/widower online support group for members of my church.

I did things alone like going to plays, movies, and national parks.

For the most part, I lived simply and slowly while serving myself and others. And in the process, I found myself.

I came to know what brings me joy. It seems so simple now, but it took time and focus and a simple life to figure it out.

I learned that these are what bring me joy:

- Loving and being loved
- Designing and creating things
- Teaching

- Writing
- Helping and serving others

So now I intentionally build these things into my life.

After almost 3 years of being alone, I remarried a wonderful woman. Mitzi is also a widow and so she shares and understands the devastating loss of a spouse. She has also pulled herself out of the depths and created a new life. I have five wonderful children whom I love dearly. I've extended my love to Mitzi's three children and her son-in-law. I have a granddaughter who makes my heart happy. I stay connected with my extended family.

I design and create software and businesses — and I write books, which I use as a way to teach, help, and serve others.

I teach at my church and mentor others on creating businesses, developing software, and creating passive income streams.

I help and serve my wife and my immediate family, my extended family, and my customers.

It's a good life. Still hard, still challenging. I still miss Tiffany and the life we expected to share, but I'm grateful to love and be loved.

I live simply, live slowly, and live intentionally by incorporating into my life the things that bring me joy. This makes my life more fulfilling and more purposeful.

What I've learned through my painful experience is what I'm trying to share with you in this book.

It's my hope that in some small and humble way, I can help you learn to have more life, more joy, and more purpose. And so I write this book and from the depth of my heart desire that you are able to catch the vision, apply it to your life, and benefit from the results.

Chapter 2

How Living Slowly Makes More Life

Living Slowly results in more life, more joy, and more purpose.

How? Glad you asked :)

Mitzi and I were fine dining at a highly-rated restaurant recently. We had a seven-course meal. The second course was a scallop. One scallop, served on a small amount of mashed potato. The mashed potato was set on a small amount of sauce.

The scallop was presented in the middle of a large plate, about 10 inches in diameter.

As Mitzi and I ate our individual scallop, we took very small bites. We savored each one. As we would take a bite, we shared what we were experiencing. The flavor, the texture. We talked about how the scallop was cooked so perfectly.

We shared how the flavor blended with the mashed potato—we'd never had the combination before. We talked about the presentation.

We ate slowly. We paid attention to every detail. We shared the experience. Without touching each other, it was still intimate.

It was a beautiful moment because we slowed down. We noticed the details. We communicated what we were experiencing. It was all about slowing down and savoring the experience.

I could have easily put the whole scallop in my mouth, taken a few bites, and swallowed all while talking about nothing, then moved on to the next thing. And if I had, I would have missed all the pleasure and joy that moment gave us.

Slowing down and noticing the details of things makes more life and brings more joy. The key is to slow down and notice. There is potential joy in so many things we do every day, but we miss out on it by moving too fast, by not noticing or paying attention.

Think back to a time when you ate something delicious and slowed down to savor it and notice the details. Perhaps you shared the experience with a loved one, which made it even more delightful. In that moment, how did you feel? Were you happier? More at peace?

When I was a young teenager, my family went camping and boating at a lake. My mom had ice in a cooler and brought a gallon of milk. In the morning, she excitedly called me over and said, "Damon, you need to taste this milk."

It was next to the ice all night and was quite chilled. She poured some for both of us. Time slowed for a few moments as we sipped that milk. We noticed the beautiful surroundings, fresh air, stillness of the early morning, and the natural coldness of the milk. Sharing that moment with my mom was so meaningful. Now, 40 years later, it still brings me joy to think about.

There is so much potential joy in so many parts of our daily lives. We miss much of it because we are so busy running to the next thing.

My mom has a small plant in her guest restroom. There is a quote on a sign next to it with a quote from Lao Tzu that says, "Nature does not hurry, yet everything is accomplished." I'd add that when we don't hurry not only is everything accomplished, it is accomplished with more joy and purpose.

Live Slowly. Slow down to notice the details. Slow down to be present with loved ones. Slow down to appreciate goodness. *Slow down to live more.*

Chapter 3

_____

Simplifying

Idea Simplifiers

When my children were young, they were so active and energetic that simply going out to eat in a restaurant was stressful. We took it as an opportunity to teach them proper and acceptable behavior.

I needed to convey to them, in the simplest terms possible, what was acceptable and unacceptable when out in public like that.

Creating a big list of rules was not going to be effective. I needed something simple that encapsulated the principle of proper behavior, something they could easily grasp, that Tiffany and I could easily communicate.

So I came up with this: "Move Slowly".

When we went out to eat, that is what I reminded them. "Please remember to move slowly."

It worked perfectly and their behavior, while not perfect, was certainly acceptable. We even, on a few occasions, got comments from other diners saying how well behaved our children were. It was a miracle :)

"Move Slowly" is an idea simplifier. It reduces an idea down to its minimal components to make it memorable and understandable, and therefore useful.

Here is another example:

Jesus was asked what is the greatest commandment. His answer: love God and love your neighbor. And then he explained that inside these two commandments fit all the law.

That is powerful!

He created an idea simplifier in which all the commandments and laws of God could fit. If you love God and love your neighbor, you will pretty much be keeping all the many commandments and laws that are meant to be kept.

If you are familiar with ancient Jewish law and how extensive it is, you will appreciate the power and genius of this idea simplifier.

Another example is the Gettysburg Address. In 264 words, Abraham Lincoln concisely stated why the Union was fighting the Civil War. This short speech has gone down in history as brilliant, memorable, and poignant. Because it was simple and concise.

The reason I'm sharing these examples with you is because the phrase "Live Slowly" is an idea simplifier. It encapsulates numerous ideas, experiences, principles, and solutions into a single phrase that is memorable and understandable, and therefore useful. It can be applied to every aspect of your life and every role you have. It will give you more joy and more purpose in your life.

Live Slowly means to slow down, appreciate the important things in life, and prioritize and value the things that bring you joy, meaning, and fulfillment.

It means to remove excess from your life. Reduce the noise and the clutter. Restructure your priorities. Create a value system where you live slowly so you can live more fully.

The Value of Simplicity

"Simplifying our lives increases the probability of achieving the most important things in life— the best things."

— Lynn G. Robbins

The value in simplifying our lives is that instead of doing good things, we do the best things. And when we do the best things, we are the happiest, most joyful, and most fulfilled.

My business partner and mentor Del Walmsley wisely says, "What gets in the way of a great life? A good life." Being okay with keeping our life as it currently is prevents us from making it better.

After Tiffany's death, I needed to heal. I needed to find myself and understand my purpose in life now that one of my primary motivations and reasons for living, was gone.

Simplifying my life was the foundation for healing and living again.

DAMON JANIS

In my case, that meant selling my house and giving everything away, reducing the amount of work I was doing, removing stresses and pressures that were optional, spending a lot of time sitting at the lake watching the ducks and thinking or sitting on the beach watching the sunrise. I visited temples and connected with God. I spent time and connected with loved ones like my children and extended family.

Simplifying gave me time and space to find myself; to understand what brings me joy and then to structure my life to include those things.

Writing brings me joy and so I've decided to write this book.

Teaching brings me joy so I teach the things I've learned from my experiences.

Helping and serving others brings me joy and so I'm writing to help and serve you.

Designing and building things brings me joy so, as a computer programmer I continue to design and build software systems. As an entrepreneur, I design and build businesses.

Doing these things at a slow pace, with no pressure or stress, and as simply as I can makes my life more fulfilling and joyful.

I was able to figure all this out because I simplified. It cleared my head so I could see. It freed up my time so I could incorporate these things into my life. You will get the same results as you simplify. That is the value of simplicity.

Simplifying Formula

Here's a simple formula for a better life:

Take the time to understand and figure out what brings you joy. Then incorporate those things into your life in a simple way.

Simplicity as a virtue has tremendous value.

As you live slowly, you will apply the virtue of simplicity directly to your life. Given the importance of it to successfully improve your life, let's take a few minutes to understand the power of simplicity.

Why is Einstein's theory of relativity so powerful and well-known? Because he simplified it down to the most basic components that express the theory: $E=mc^2$

Finding the simplest way to express an idea is not an easy thing to do. It takes work, and it's so worth it.

Simplifying your life will reduce noise and clutter, worthless or low value activities, and free up your mind to see clearly and feel peace.

To simplify your life, start by identifying the things that really matter. Identify the key components that make a difference, then remove the things that don't matter.

Here's an example of its power:

There is an excellent book about developing a solid and lasting marriage relationship: *How to Avoid Falling in Love with a Jerk* by John Van Epp. In it, he simplifies the development of a healthy relationship into what he calls the RAM: Relationship Attachment Model.

The model consists of five elements involved in developing relationships, and each element to the left is to be more fully developed than the element to its right. The five elements are: Know, Trust, Rely, Commit, and Touch.

Van Epp explains that the Relationship Attachment Model "summarizes massive amounts of theory and research on love, attachment, intimacy, and bonding into just one interactive picture."

It's brilliant and super helpful because it's simple and easy to remember. Thousands of marriage relationships are stronger because Van Epp simplified.

Where you simplify your life, you improve your life.

Simplicity or Complexity

Simplicity compared to complexity can be the difference between success and failure. Years ago Mark Twain and Samuel Langley learned this the hard way, in two separate events.

Mark Twain invested heavily in a machine called the Paige Compositor, an extremely complex machine designed to automate the laborious task of typesetting for printing. Because of its complexity, it broke down a lot and cost a lot of money to build with all the parts it required. It was difficult to reproduce.

A competing design, the Linotype, was much simpler. It had fewer parts and fewer things that could go wrong, and it was easier to use. The Paige Compositor was a commercial failure while the Linotype was a commercial success. Twain lost all the money he invested and Paige, the inventor, died penniless. If Paige had done the hard work of creating a simple design, his invention very well could have been a commercial success.

Samuel Langley was a contemporary of the Wright brothers. He was commissioned by Congress to build a flying machine. He had all the credentials and experience that made Congress confident he could do it and was given a large budget to work with.

Unhappily, the flying machine he designed and tested, the Aerodrome, was complex. It had a lot of parts and took a long time to build and repair. It was heavy and expensive. And on top of all of that, it never worked when tested with humans on board. On the first attempt a wing clipped the catapult and the plane plunged into the river. On the second and last attempt, the plane broke up as soon as it left the catapult because of the weight and complexity.

In contrast, the Wright brothers had a small budget. They studied how birds fly and they simplified those principles into just the essential elements needed for a machine to fly under control. Their design was minimal and *simple*—and it worked!

Complexity in our lives can burden us just as the Paige Compositor and the Aerodrome were burdened. Too many parts, too much weight, too rigid and inflexible. They crumbled under their own weight.

If your life is complex, it's very difficult to be happy and to feel peace. The solution is to *simplify your life*.

Making Things Simple

You can make just about anything simpler than it currently is.

Take for example the clothes in your closet. Can you reduce the choices you have to make when you get dressed? Can you organize your clothes in a way that makes it faster and easier to get what you want?

What about the activities your children are involved in. Can you eliminate some?

Look at the stuff you own. Would your life be simpler if you had less? There would be fewer things that break that need to be fixed, and less maintenance to keep things working.

Look at your relationships. Have you let someone into your life without boundaries, so there is chaos and unpredictability? Are there relationships you could eliminate or take a step back from?

Look at your time and activities. Do you run from one thing to the next? Do you pack your schedule full of many good things, instead of just a few of the best things?

Creating complexity is easy. It seems to come naturally to most of us. Making things simple, however, takes work because we have to think through what is relevant and what isn't. We need to know what's valuable to us and what's not. Removing the parts that aren't important leaves us with just the parts that matter.

Look at how you manage your money. How many cars do you own? How much busy work do you do just to look busy? What are you really accomplishing?

The key to making things simple is actually simple itself: take a few minutes and think it through. What are you doing? What is valuable to you? What could be more efficient? Don't just act out on your emotions; think about it logically.

I know a family with young children who recently got a puppy. It seemed like a good idea at the time and it was exciting to provide their small children with a pet that was so cute and adorable.

However, after a few weeks of agonizing reality, they had to give the puppy away. It was too much work, the children got bored within a few days, and what felt like a fun thing turned out to be a big pain for the parents.

There are so many things you do each day on autopilot. Start questioning your decisions and think of ways to make things simpler.

I heard a story some years ago that goes like this:

At Thanksgiving, a mom cut her turkey in half and cooked it in the oven. Her young daughter said, "Mom, why do you cut the turkey in half?" Her mom said, "Because my mom did."

So the girl asked her grandma, "Grandma, why do you cut the turkey in half?"

The grandma replied, "Because my mom did."

So she asked her great grandma, "Why did you cut the turkey in half?"

The great grandma said, "Oh, because my oven was so small I couldn't fit the whole thing in it."

That story makes me smile and laugh every time.

How often do we do things just because that's how it's done? Every day, week, month, and year, we do things without thinking about why we are doing them or if it even makes sense.

Making things simple is simply done by thinking about why, what, and how you do things.

Chapter 4

Know Yourself

Who Am I?

I had a meeting with 50 entrepreneurs who were seeking spiritual guidance in their work. Near the end of the meeting, we were asked by the facilitator to randomly select a number from 1 to 150. Then we were asked to open the Old Testament to that chapter in Psalms and read through it, seeing what stood out to us and sharing if we wanted.

One of the participants picked the number 77. Once she read Psalms 77, she shared some profound thoughts based on verse 6. It resonated with me and helped me see the importance of understanding who we are.

Psalms 77:6 reads, "I commune with my own heart and my spirit makes a diligent search."

She then said, "God wants us to know who we are and it's not wrong to commune with yourself. God wants us to know who we are and *needs* us to know who we are and *we need* to know who we are. If we are going to do what he wants us to do, and if we're going to fulfill our purpose, we have to know who we are. It doesn't work if you don't know. *It's not fulfilling your purpose if you have no idea who you are.*"

Coming to know myself was a key part of putting my life together again. Understanding will enable more life, more joy, and more purpose.

How to Learn Who You Are

You are unique and individual. Nobody is exactly like you. So who are you, really?

The best way to figure out who you are is to create a heart list: a list of things that bring you joy and make your heart happy. When you do them they make something resonate inside your soul. You feel happy, you feel peace, you feel joy.

After you create your heart list, go to each item on the list and ask yourself, "Why does this bring me joy?" Then, go back to each one and dig down a couple more layers. Take your initial answer and ask why again. Then take that answer and ask why.

As you write your heart list and question each item, you'll uncover who you really are. You'll understand your core and discover who you are beneath the physical veneer—you'll see your heart and soul.

This can be a scary thing to do. Many of us go through life not really understanding who we are, and being afraid of what we might find if we looked any deeper. Please don't let this deter you. You are a beautiful person with gifts and intelligence and value.

The point of discovering who you truly are is not to pass judgment on whether you are good or bad. The point is simply to *know yourself* in order to create happiness and peace in your life.

When you know who you are, you can understand your purpose in life. And understanding your purpose gives you meaning, which gives you direction and hope and purpose.

Once you understand what brings you joy, improve the joy in your life by intentionally adding more things from your heart list. Every day, choose to do at least one thing on your heart list.

Chapter 5

_____

Slowing Down

You Don't Have to Do Everything

There is a famous episode of _I Love Lucy_ in which Lucy and Ethel are working in a chocolate factory on the assembly line. Their boss says if one candy gets past them and into the packing room unwrapped, they will be fired.

As chocolates come down the assembly line faster and faster, Lucy and Ethel try to keep up. It's impossible and they start stuffing chocolates into their mouths, their shirts, and their hats. When their boss comes in it looks like they've handled everything fine, so she yells to the operator, "Speed it up!"

While everything looked fine, it wasn't.

If we fill our life with so many activities, so many responsibilities, and so much work, we can't keep up. We end up doing nothing well and it will eventually overwhelm us.

Stress significantly rises when we can't keep up. More stress impacts our physical and mental health. It removes joy.

So, be careful to only take on what you can handle.

If you are suffering in any way and feel overwhelmed, cut things out of your life. Restructure and reduce. Simplify. Declutter. So say "no" to more things and more activities.

Just because someone asks you to do something for them doesn't mean you must. It's okay to politely decline.

This includes your adult children.

I belong to a private widow/widower online support group. Recently, a widower posted that his daughter is married to a man who will not work. All he does is play video games. Together, they have a small baby.

This kind widower moved into their basement so he could help pay the utilities, watch the baby, and give them support. However, he was struggling because his son-in-law quit his job and hadn't bothered to get a new one. His daughter wanted to go back to school, but they couldn't afford it and the widower was paying all the bills.

In response, I shared some harsh but what I believe is healthy advice, based on personal and painful experience:

It's really hard to see our adult children suffer. We want to intervene and alleviate the suffering and protect them. The healthiest thing to do is go live your own life and not enmesh your life with that of your SIL and daughter. Your daughter will need to figure out what to do and that is a terrible position for her to be in, but she's an adult and she gets to figure it out. You can't fix this problem and it's not really yours to fix anyway. Detach, with love :)

If you are in this kind of situation, please take care of yourself and let your adult children take care of themselves. It's part of applying Live Slowly to your life.

The 80/20 Principle for Slowing Down

In the late 1800s, Italian economist Vilfredo Pareto was studying the economies of past countries and civilizations. He made an interesting observation. In every case, regardless of political structure, social structure, or any other factors, about 20% of the population controlled about 80% of the land and wealth.

Much later, management consultant Joseph M. Hiram suggested it as a principle and named it the Pareto Principle.

The principle is essentially this: roughly 80% of effects come from 20% of causes.

Here are some examples of what this means:

+ Look at where you go in your house. You likely go to 20% of your house 80% of the time.

+ Look at all the seats in your car. You likely use 20% of the seats 80% of the time.

- Think about the types of food that you eat. You probably eat the same 20% of foods about 80% of the time.

- Consider all the restaurants you visit. You likely go to the same 20%, 80% of the time.

- Here's one I think about each time I shave my face with a razor and shaving cream. 80% of the surface of the face (cheeks and neck) takes about 20% of the time. And 20% of the surface area (around the mouth and nose) takes about 80% of the time :)

You see the 80/20 principle all over when you become aware of it.

You can harness the power of this principle to effectively simplify your life. Use it to:

- Significantly increase your productivity
- Significantly improve your relationships
- Significantly simplify your life
- *Live Slowly*

You may have heard the phrase, "small hinges swing big doors." If you picture two small metal hinges on a huge wooden castle door, you can get a visual of what the 80/20 principle looks like.

Look for the small hinges that swing the big doors in your life.

For example, here is a simple formula for having more peace in your life:

Reduce your load by 20% and your stress level will reduce by 80%.

The reason for this is that 80% of the stress you feel in your life is coming from 20% of the causes of that stress.

If you focus on reducing the 20% of causes, you will significantly reduce your level of stress. You don't have to remove all the causes, just the ones that create the most stress.

Here are a few more examples of how the 80/20 principle can be applied:

+ In the restaurant business, there are only two factors that account for the majority of the expenses: labor and food. If you want to improve the health of a restaurant, the place to start is looking at the labor costs and the food costs. That's where you'll find the small hinges that swing big doors. You'll find the 20% of the causes of 80% of the effects.

+ In many businesses, 20% of the customers create 80% of the headaches and hassle and problems that you have to deal with. So, if you want to simplify your business, make more money and work less, "fire" the worst 20% of your customers and your negative hassles will reduce by a whopping 80%.

+ In interpersonal relationships, it's likely that 20% of the relationships in your life cause you 80% of the negativity and hassle you experience. If you focus on restructuring those few relationships, you will see an 80% improvement.

Let's look at how you can apply the Live Slowly idea simplifier in your life by applying the 80/20 principle:

If you are feeling overwhelmed it's likely that there are only a couple of primary factors in your life that, if readjusted, would significantly reduce that feeling.

If you are constantly busy and anxious, it's likely there are only a couple of primary factors that are the main reasons for you not feeling calm or peace.

What are those couple of primary factors? When you identify them and you work on re-factoring them, you are leveraging the Live Slowly principle significantly.

DAMON JANIS

Live Slowly in Every Part of Your Life

One morning, while contemplating the Live Slowly idea simplifier, it occurred to me how it applies everywhere in our lives.

Ideas started pouring into my head and I wrote them down as quickly as I could. When the ideas stopped flowing, I realized how comprehensive this idea simplifier is.

You can apply it to being a parent, a student, a leader, a child, a spouse, an employer, and an employee. Every hat you wear in your life can benefit from applying Live Slowly.

I hope to write a series of Live Slowly books that apply the idea to a variety of life roles and experiences. Here are some of my ideas (maybe some of these are available now!):

- ✦ Living again after your spouse dies
- ✦ Being the parent of a drug addict
- ✦ Holding productive meetings
- ✦ Building healthy relationships

- Succeeding at work
- Managing a to-do list
- Starting a new business
- Running a business
- Leading a business
- Designing a business
- Systemizing a business
- Teaching
- Making effective decisions
- Writing books
- Deepening your spirituality
- Learning how to learn
- Creating effective daily routines and habits
- Creating passive income streams
- Retiring in five years or less
- Designing and building software
- Grieving loved ones
- Finding purpose in life
- Simplifying

- Thinking more clearly and effectively
- Being more productive
- Remarrying after death of spouse
- Traveling
- Vacationing
- The 80/20 principle

These are areas of my life where I've benefited from applying Live Slowly. Even in my efforts to write about all of this I will apply the Live Slowly principle. For example, I'm satisfied that I came up with this realization of how Live Slowly applies to so much. I'm satisfied seeing the list I came up with. I'm satisfied if I never write any of these books and I won't beat myself up over it.

If I write one book, I'll be satisfied. If I write them all I'll be satisfied.

If it helps one person, I'll be satisfied. If it helps a million people, I'll be satisfied.

Writing is a lot of work. It's hard to take an idea, simplify it, and communicate it in a clear and concise way.

So, every step will be celebrated and appreciated. I don't feel any pressure to get this done quickly or even finish it before I die.

If any of these topics sound interesting to you, check if they've been written. If they have, I hope you enjoy and benefit from them.

Addicted to Complexity

Some of us are addicted to making our lives complex and difficult. While it can often feel like making things more complex is equal to being more productive, in reality, complexity just makes productivity more difficult.

Here are some examples of how this addiction exhibits itself:

* You create a long list of all the things you need to get done today. At the end of the day, you didn't get everything done and you feel like your day was a failure.

* When you get burned out doing things for other people and giving of yourself, instead of taking some time out to take care of yourself, you think you are inadequate for feeling burned out.

* When you feel tired and need to rest, you kick yourself for it.

* When you unexpectedly realize your life is calm and peaceful, you

immediately create some work or chaos or complexity in your life which takes away that calm and peace.

+ When you plan an activity, you put great value on things that take a lot of work but that, in actuality, do not add any or much value to the activity.

The bottom line is that if you are uncomfortable feeling calm, you may be addicted to complexity. This is a perfectly normal and common human experience.

Many of us carry pain, fear, and regrets. When we are calm, we become more aware of those unpleasant feelings, so it's natural to stir up some complexity in our life to distract ourselves. We don't usually do it on purpose. It's a natural response to avoid something unpleasant and we do it without thinking.

Are you addicted to complexity?

It's okay if you don't get everything done today on your to-do list. It really is okay. You may get just one or two important things done today—

that's enough. You can end the day feeling good that you got the most important things done.

If you are burned out, it's okay to slow down and take care of yourself.

If you are tired, it's okay to rest.

If you are stressed out, it's okay to restructure your life to remove and reduce the most intense causes of that stress.

If you have lots of drama in your life, it's okay to restructure your life to remove it, regardless of whether you are creating it or others are.

There is always a way to make things better than they are, even if it's just a little better at first. You can always start.

You will have fears about stopping the complexity, but you will find that as you simplify and let go, it will be okay. Even better than okay; it will be great!

If you're addicted to complexity, adopt the Live Slowly principle and slow down, breathe, and allow peace into your life by simplifying.

Don't Should All Over Yourself

When my daughter was recovering from drug addiction, I met with her and her counselor at the rehab clinic. Her counselor shared this idea simplifier that I found quite profound.

She said to my daughter, "Don't should all over yourself."

It made me smile. It's funny and memorable and it perfectly expresses how we can be gentle on ourselves and give ourselves love.

There is no need to beat ourselves up for things we've done—for our imperfections and weaknesses, and failings.

We don't need to hold ourselves to such a high standard that we can't succeed and therefore feel like a failure and then give up and self-destruct. It's okay to set lower expectations for ourselves that are more realistic and do-able.

Be easy on, and love, yourself.

Being Busy Is Not Being Productive

We need to address a common misperception that is running rampant in our culture. Many people think that if they are busy doing things they are, therefore, productive.

This may have been true in the past, but it's not anymore. There are so many ways to look and be busy now. Attention spans are shorter. Information is thrown at us in vast quantities.

I don't watch the news, but recently, while eating breakfast at a hotel, they had a news channel on. So much was happening on the display: there were people talking, two news tickers scrolling and several boxes flashing information.

I remembered how, in my younger years, a newscast was just a person talking and that's all that was on the screen. It occurred to me that we are just overloaded with information and things trying to grab our attention—on something as mundane as a news report—that it's more distracting than actually productive.

No one can absorb that much information at once.

We can be busy all day long. Driving around. Doing social media. Sending off and reading text messages. How much of that is important? How much of that really matters?

The point I'm making is that to have a more fulfilling and joyful life, we need to recognize the difference between doing things that make us busy and doing things that actually matter.

If we are busy and not productive, we feel overwhelmed easier. Something inside us knows we are wasting time. It's unfulfilling.

Being busy and unproductive is a distraction from knowing who you are and doing important and meaningful things.

Author and thought leader Charles Duhigg studies productivity and has this to say:

> At the core of productivity is the feeling that you are doing the work that matters to you most at the moment you most want

to do it, without having to make huge sacrifices along the way.

So we need to unbundle the notions of productivity and busyness. Even in the 1950s, if you were busy eight hours a day that probably meant you were productive for eight hours of the day. And today, even if you're busy 14 hours a day, you might not ever get anything important done.

The number of ways that we can be distracted, or the different channels for 'busyness' have now exploded. That means it's easier to feel overwhelmed and feel busy. (Webb, 2017)

Hustling Is Overrated

When I played Little League baseball as a child, one of my coaches would yell at us to "hustle." That was his answer to everything. If we would just hustle more, we'd be winners :)

I've since learned that it isn't necessary to hustle. Life is more peaceful when we don't, and we actually get more done.

Do you know anyone who hustles all the time? Maybe it's you.

Hustling is being busy all the time. Moving quickly, keeping the pauses between tasks at a minimum. The problem is that it prevents thinking. Action without prior thought and planning is wasted.

Wise parents teach their children to think before they act. Consider these:

> *"For every minute spent in organizing, an hour is earned."*
>
> — Benjamin Franklin

"Every minute you spend in planning saves 10 minutes in execution; this gives you a 1,000 percent Return on Energy!"

— Brian Tracy

"Every minute spent planning, is a minute not spent practicing being impromptu."

— zastels on Reddit

Thinking and planning remove the need for hustling.

Many mornings before I get out of bed I do the following:

+ Say a prayer
+ Read from a book written before the printing press was created
+ Write down something I'm grateful for
+ Write down a question I have and then whatever thoughts come into my head as I think about it
+ Review my short, mid, and long-term goals

- Write down a to-do list that does at least one step, even if it's small, to move toward accomplishing my goals
- Organize my to-do list in order of importance

During the day, I just focus on getting the most important things done. It might only be 1, 2, or 3 things in the whole day. I don't worry about getting everything done, just the most important ones.

The result? I don't hustle, but I'm extremely effective because I'm doing the most valuable things.

To the outside world, it doesn't look like I'm doing much. I don't run around during the day. When I drive somewhere, I'm relaxed. When I'm working, I'm relaxed. When I'm talking to my wife or children, I'm relaxed and tuned in. Why? Because I'm not hustling and I don't need to.

You'll make more money by planning and being intentional in what you do, than by hustling.

You'll build stronger relationships by being present with loved ones than by hustling. You'll feel more peace and happiness in your life by moving slowly than by hustling.

In Mitch Albom's *Tuesdays with Morrie*, Morrie is an aging college professor. As his body is slowly dying, a past student comes to visit him each Tuesday. As they visit, Morrie shares profound insights. I share my favorite quotes in a chapter later in this book, but one in particular is relevant here:

> 'Part of the problem, Mitch, is that everyone is in such a hurry,' Morrie said. 'People haven't found meaning in their lives, so they're running all the time looking for it. They think the next car, the next house, the next job. Then they find those things are empty, too, and they keep running.' (Albom, 1997, p. 136)

All of us have done this at one point or another. We've run around buying stuff, looking for meaning in our lives. Things, however, don't add meaning to our lives. They are empty.

When we seek meaning in our life through hustling to have more stuff, more success, more praise, more fame, we won't find meaning. Instead we'll be singing that tune, "And I still haven't found what I'm looking for."

Ben Shewry, chef at the 33rd best restaurant in the world, has learned that hustling for success isn't what matters.

> When I was younger, I was very interested in trying to achieve a certain level of success, winning a lot of awards and reaching a level of recognition from my peers. As you grow older you realize that the things that really matter to you are your friends and your family. It doesn't matter to them whether or not my restaurant is ranked number 33 in the world. They only care really if I'm a decent human being, and that I treat my wife and my children and my family and my friends with respect. (McGinn, 2015)

Hustling is overrated.

Create Margin in Your Life

Margin is the space between boundaries. You are probably familiar with margins for books— the space between the boundary of the words and the outer edge of the page.

The concept of margin in life is similar and important to understand. If you don't have margin in your life, you can suffer burn-out, stress, and feeling overwhelmed.

I remember reading Truett Cathy's autobiography—the founder of Chick-Fil-A. He had his restaurants close on Sunday because the employees needed a rest, as did the equipment.

Nature itself naturally has margin everywhere. Lions don't hunt 100% of the time. After they have a successful hunt and are filled, they lay around and rest, letting their bodies digest their food. There is a time to hunt, a time to eat, and a time to rest.

There is margin between storms and between seasons as well. The earth has margin between winters. In *The Lion, The Witch, and the Wardrobe*, there is a 100-year winter and what happens? Stagnation. Nature stagnated and couldn't regenerate because there was no margin. While imaginary, that's what would happen if the earth didn't have margin between the seasons. Everywhere in nature, we see margin that allows the earth and the beings and plants and animals on it to rest and regenerate.

Just like in a business and of course, in nature, all people need a break to rest and recharge, and that's where margin comes in.

Think about where you live. Is your bed in the middle of your kitchen? No. We design boundaries into our living spaces. We use walls, dividers, and space between furniture to delineate the margins. Can you imagine living in a space where the kitchen has a bed in the middle of it and a toilet next to the kitchen sink? We create margin in our living spaces so each space can function properly.

We create margin between us and our neighbors. Property boundaries, fences, walls, landscaping are all used to put margin into our lives. The margin specifies the boundaries we need and want from others.

Have you ever talked to someone you don't know very well, who violates your personal space and causes you to feel uncomfortable? You feel uncomfortable because there is no margin.

I recently took Mitzi to a very nice restaurant and we noticed there was a lot of margin between the tables. It made for a quiet and relaxing dining experience. The less margin, the less quiet and less relaxing. More margin equals more peace. The same thing happens in our lives.

There is a time to work, a time to play, a time to rest, and a time to worship. There's a time to plan, a time to learn or to run, walk, or sleep. There is a time and a season for everything in our lives. We are less effective if we are always "on" —working or playing. We need margin between the activities in our life.

If you live your life without margin, I hope reading this section makes you aware of it. Once you are aware of it, you can intentionally create margin in your life and find more peace and happiness.

Margin is necessary to recharge, reflect, learn, and understand. It's an opportunity for our minds to rest so we can think more clearly.

As a software programmer for over 30 years, I have experienced the need for margin many many times. There are many times when I'll be deeply concentrating on a tough problem that I can't figure out. Eventually, I will admit to being totally stuck—no solution in sight and I have no idea how to find it. So, I step away from my computer and create margin by talking to my wife, taking a walk, riding my bike, and totally stop thinking about the problem I was trying to solve.

There are usually two outcomes to this. One is that I'll be thinking about something totally unrelated when an idea pops into my head on how to solve the problem. The other is that I go to sleep and when I wake up in the morning, or sometimes in the middle of the night, with the answer.

The margin is necessary to find the solution. On the surface, it doesn't make sense that we need to stop and do something else to find a solution or answer, but that's just how it works, so embrace it.

Margin gives space for healing. When we are sick, we heal faster if we create margin.

I recently watched a *Chef's Table* episode (Fried, 2015) featuring Niki Nakayama who created the wonderful restaurant n/naka in Los Angeles. When I went to make a reservation, I found that you have to reserve three months in advance, and there is no availability otherwise. They open up reservations on Sunday at 10AM for 3 months ahead and it immediately fills up.

In the episode, Niki spoke about how she opened a sushi restaurant before n/naka. The restaurant was successful, but she felt burned out. It was very technically great, but it wasn't a reflection of who she is, so she decided to sell the restaurant, even though she had no idea what she was going to do next. For the next several months, she took some time and reflected on what she really wanted and how she could create something that fit with who she is. Finally, inspiration came and she created n/naka. What I realized is that she intentionally created margin in her life, which enabled her to get the inspiration for something great.

After Tiffany's death, I intentionally created margin in my life as well. That's what sitting at the lakes for hours watching ducks was about. That's what visiting the temples of my church was about. Creating that margin lead me to understand the life I wanted to create.

You may not have the ability to stop working. If you are a caretaker, you may need to keep caretaking. You may have young children that require a lot of time and attention. That doesn't mean you can't create margin in your life. You can always create margin somewhere.

Do you get to go to the bathroom? Of course you do. What if you take an extra five or 10 minutes in there and give yourself some margin. When you lay down to sleep at night, go to bed a few minutes earlier and give yourself some margin.

Creating margin is slowing down. Create it between the tasks you do, so when you complete a task, take a break. When you finish an activity, don't immediately start the next one. Build some margin into your life. When you complete a project, create margin— celebrate the completion before you start your next project. When you end one meeting (and ending five to ten minutes early won't upset anyone), take some margin before starting the next one.

Create margin between events in your life. Everything from the micro events like taking bites of food, to the macro events like taking some time off work every once-in-a-while allow you to build margin into your life at any time of the day and in any situation.

Dr. Richard A. Swenson, physician and researcher, observes that the world is in pain. As a physician, he sees patients every 15 minutes in his medical practice. They are anxious, depressed, stressed, and drained. He says:

> They suffer from a lack of margin in their lives. There is no peace. No quiet. No time between this event and that event, this responsibility, and that responsibility. We go from program to program to program without ever taking a deep breath. We're weighed down so much by the number of bricks that have been piled in our backpack that we're about to fall backward and roll back down the hill we've climbed up in life. (as cited in Trimble, n.d.)

How can you create margin?

Ride your bike.

Take a walk.

Sit still.

Have a nap.

Schedule breaks in your schedule.

Say no to things people ask you to do.

Say no to things you are thinking of doing.

Stop doing less valuable things.

Simplify your schedule.

Simplify your activities.

Get rid of junk in your house.

Declutter.

Figure out what is actually important and valuable and just do that.

Mindful Tasks

Modern innovations relieve us from mundane tasks our ancestors had to do. The abundant resources we enjoy make life more comfortable with less work. There is a downside, though. We have lost some of the joy that comes from doing mundane tasks.

When my children read this chapter, I'm sure they will be confused. They see me correctly as someone who is constantly finding ways to avoid mundane tasks. I hire people to maintain my yard and instead of personally helping someone move, I prefer to hire a few people who need and want the work and contribute that way.

When Mitzi and I were getting to know each other, I let her know right up front that I don't do manual labor. I don't do yard work, gardening, moving, or house repairs. That was odd to her because she enjoys vacuuming her house, gardening, and trimming the bushes in the yard. She gets joy from these simple and mundane tasks.

Nevertheless, we got married with the understanding that I wouldn't do manual labor tasks and she was fine with that.

Interestingly, since we've been married, I have replaced several broken light switches, replaced the garage opener light bulbs, installed an electronic lock on the front door, fixed the garage door, and moved furniture around to accommodate guests.

It's interesting because I actually found joy in doing these things. I think the joy came from helping and serving others, feeling useful, and accomplishing something that created more value in our lives.

I'm a work in progress on this principle of doing mundane tasks.

Five years ago at a conference, a successful entrepreneur who travels with her two young daughters gave everyone a tip. She encouraged us to find people to do the mundane tasks of life so we have more time to do things that make money. As an example, she told us she has a chef who travels with her and her children. The chef takes care of all their food needs. At the time, I thought that was pretty cool because she freed up time that would normally be spent meal planning, prepping and serving.

Now, I have more experience. I look at her advice and think twice. Perhaps she's missing out on something more productive and valuable than making money. How would her joy increase if she spent some time each day serving her children in a useful way, and spending time with them by doing the mundane but mindful task of food planning and preparing with them?

My paternal grandfather Sid Janofsky owned a deli in the 1940's in Los Angeles. He cooked a wonderful brisket and made delicious brisket sandwiches. In the 1970's, we would visit his house in Redwood City, CA where he lived on a waterfront property. He had a boat dock and we would go there and water ski. He made his brisket sandwiches and we loved them. And loved him for making them for us.

A few years ago, I decided to recreate and perfect his brisket sandwich. I made 26 briskets over a one-and-a-half-year period. I documented each brisket experiment and how it was prepped, spiced, and cooked. I tried sandwiches with different breads, condiments, and styles.

I can't even express how fun this was. I've made brisket sandwiches for friends and family and totally enjoyed it. I even thought perhaps I'd open a restaurant that just sells these wonderful brisket sandwiches. But I realized that I'm doing it for the joy of making sandwiches and entertaining, not for money. I'll be the grandpa known and loved for making great brisket sandwiches. What can be better than that? Every time I make a brisket for my family or friends, it's an act of love and it gives me joy.

The simple mindful task of cooking can be a joy. The simple task of straightening up a room can be a joy. Can gardening bring joy? I never liked gardening when I worked in the garden as a child. Now as an adult, after learning about how mindful tasks can bring joy, maybe I should try it!

Instead of trying to avoid "mindless" tasks, what if we see them as "mindful" ones and embrace them?

I was recently watching *Cooked*, a documentary series that features author Michael Pollan experimenting with different types of cooking. There is a part where Samin Nosrat is making a simple meal from scratch. She's cutting vegetables, collecting herbs from a plant, and putting them together in a pot of boiling water. As she works, she says:

> These are some of my favorite things to do. You might think of it as mindless tasks but I like to think of it as *mindful* tasks. It's about getting to that point in your own mind where this becomes pleasure instead of drudgery. (2016, 44:05)

She continues:

As a culture we've just gotten so far away from these little tasks it seems like it's getting in the way of life. But actually this is life. What better thing than to be doing the thing where your hand is in the pot. Anything where people are actually working and doing something and making something, I think that's among the most valuable things we can do as humans. (2016, 44:36)

Mindful tasks are not getting in the way of life. They *are* life!

Stress Indicators

Being aware of stress indicators in your life will help you slow down.

My dad teaches dentistry at two dental schools. He retired from private practice years ago and now, at 81 years old, finds joy in helping young dental students learn from his vast experience.

He recently did a research project with a couple of students. They tested the bonding strength of a bridge my dad designed compared to the standard bridge design most dentists use. They put the bridges in a machine that pulls it apart slowly and under observable conditions. I'm happy to report that my dad's design was three times stronger than the conventional design. But that's beside the point here.

What I want to point out is that before the bond broke, there were indications that it was going to break. Cracks and stress marks would appear.

There are always signs of stress.

Our cars have indicators in them for things like low air pressure, too much heat, and too much speed. They can warn us of impending failure so we can take corrective action before failure actually occurs.

Our bodies have these indicators too. When I was Tiffany's caretaker and her life was on the line with the treatment decisions we had to make, it was extremely stressful. My body responded with intense pain in my lower abdomen.

On Thanksgiving 2013, I was in the emergency room because the pain in my abdomen was so intense. They did all kinds of tests and couldn't find anything wrong. They gave me some pain medicine and sent me out.

The pain would come and go. I went to five different doctors and after months of trying to find the problem, I finally visited a veteran doctor at the Mayo Clinic in Scottsdale. After reviewing my history, past exams, and tests, and doing his own evaluation, he couldn't find anything wrong either. Then he shared something so insightful, I hope it will help you too.

He said that when he was in medical school in the late 60's they had a class on stress and how it affects the body. He explained that the body can experience heightened pain in a stressful situation. He learned that sometimes there isn't any physical reason why someone feels pain.

Understanding the stress I was experiencing being Tiffany's caregiver and having my cherished wife's life hanging in the balance, he attributed the discomfort I was having to stress. His recommendation was, to the best of my ability, reduce that stress. I had to think about that one. How can you reduce stress in a prolonged, life-threatening situation?

My conclusion was that to reduce the stress, I needed to simply accept things I didn't have control over. As I started working on that, the stress reduced. It didn't go away, of course, but it did lessen significantly. And as my stress reduced by accepting what I couldn't control, I started to feel better physically. Accepting what we can't control is another aspect of living slowly.

Listen to your body, your mind, and your soul to notice indicators that are giving you a warning. Heed these indicators before burn-out occurs.

Indications that you are stressed out and on a path to burnout are varied. Here are a few that indicate you need to slow down:

+ No tolerance for unexpected events.
+ Lack of patience with loved ones.
+ Excessive worry about things you can't control.
+ Body health indicators.
+ Heightened emotions that feel or are out of control.
+ Unable to think or reason clearly.

A great teacher and church leader, Jeffrey R. Holland, in a general church-wide talk called "Like A Broken Vessel," shared this profound advice and insight:

In preventing illness whenever possible, watch for the stress indicators in yourself and in others you may be able to help. As with your automobile, be alert to rising temperatures, excessive speed, or a tank low on fuel. When you face 'depletion depression,' make the requisite adjustments. Fatigue is the common enemy of us all—so slow down, rest up, replenish, and refill. Physicians promise us that if we do not take time to be well, we most assuredly will take time later on to be ill.

Following the Live Slowly principles will help you heal and be well.

Chapter 6

Lessons from Tiffany

Since Tiffany's death, I've come to realize some profound insights. A death of a loved one, especially a spouse, readjusts your focus and refines your perspective.

Having gone through that experience, I've learned to see life through a more effective lens. The lessons I share in this chapter come from deep grief and pain, much soul searching with eyes open and a yearning to see. They form the core of the Live Slowly way.

Life is filled with opposites. Out of joy comes pain, and conversely out of pain comes joy. When you marry the love of your life and your best friend, there is joy. Inevitably, however, one of you will die and that will bring pain. But the pain could not have existed without the joy first.

When a mother brings a child into the world, there is pain in the carrying and delivery and birth. Then there is joy in the new life that is created. Without the pain of childbirth, there wouldn't be the joy of receiving new life.

There was and is sadness and struggle in Tiffany's death, so it follows that goodness and learning come from it as well. Here is some of the goodness and learning I have benefited from that I'd like to share with you.

Love is the most important thing in the world

The first thing I learned from Tiffany's death was directly from her. Two weeks before she died and as her body was withering away from cancer, she wrote a letter to one of our children. At the end of the letter she said, "I think that love is the most important thing in the world and that's what we're here to do; to learn how to love and I'm enjoying that so much!"

Stop always chasing the 'next great thing'

Too many of us live in anticipation of 'the next great thing.' Why can't we celebrate the great things we already have?

How many great things have you already accomplished and received in life? Do you feel all the joy and satisfaction you expected to feel before you had it? Your life is passing you by if you don't stop and take the time to be fully joyful and satisfied in the things that used to be 'the next great thing' but are now in the past.

Life can end suddenly and unexpectedly. It will end for each of us sometime. Let's not waste it by always chasing the 'next great thing.' Keep moving forward, and also be content.

You've already won the lottery

Do you realize how wonderful it is to be alive? It's a miracle and a gift. There are so many systems in your body that must function to keep us alive. Even when some things are going wrong, nearly everything is going right.

With a few exceptions, most people can see, hear, and taste—and if you can't do all three, you can likely do most of them. And anyone reading this can love, be loved, and think. Just being alive is having won the lottery.

Focusing on what matters makes life worth living

We choose what we focus on. I've learned that focusing on the things that matter make my life worth living.

After Tiffany's death, my desire to keep living was sometimes weak. My motivation and purpose in life seemed to evaporate with her death.

As I've figured out what really matters and the things that really make a difference, and I've focused on them, my desire for living has significantly increased. When you Live Slowly, you bring into focus those things that really matter and that make life worth living.

Most people are not satisfied with their life

This is a sad truth. I think it has to do with always chasing after the next great thing, not understanding what actually matters, or not understanding who we are and what makes us tick.

Since Tiffany's death, I've come to realize that way too many of us are not satisfied. This doesn't need to be. There can be so much more satisfaction in life by applying the Live Slowly principles. Be content.

Being #1 is overrated

We don't have to be number one, or beat the next person, or make X amount of money more than someone else. What does it really matter? What does it count for? There are 7 billion people on the earth. Do you really have to be number one to be satisfied and content?

There isn't anything lasting or meaningful about being number one. It's an arbitrary comparison that we tend to put great value in, but in truth has very little value. It's amazing how much effort people will put into it, though. And all for what? When they get there, are they satisfied for the rest of their life? Does it improve their relationships with loved ones?

When I was in college, I was considered poor, yet I had a car, made $7/hr (this was 1989), never went hungry, and had a clean (yet tiny) place to live. While I often thought of myself as poor, compared to families I worked with as a missionary in Brazil, I would be considered well-off.

It's so false to compare ourselves to anyone else. I know it's human nature, and probably not possible to avoid, but it's really pointless and futile. We compare ourselves to those around us and feel good if we come out on top and bad if we come out on the bottom.

This happens in sports all the time. Someone is always better, faster, or stronger than you. When you compete in a group where everyone is worse, slower, or weaker than you, you feel like a winner, but if you performed exactly the same against better players, you'd feel like a big loser. Your skill never changed, but by comparing yourself to others, you completely change your experience. Unfortunately, there's always another group. It's a false perception when you think you are number one because you might be #1 in your 'world,' but your world has false boundaries on it. It just doesn't mean anything.

I love the book *Tuesdays with Morrie* and I'll share more about what I've learned from it in the next chapter, but for now, I want to look at what Morrie said about being number one. I loved this when I read it:

It is 1979, a basketball game in the Brandeis gym. The team is doing well, and the student section begins a chant, "We're number one! We're number one!" Morrie is sitting nearby. He is puzzled by the cheer. At one point, in the midst of "We're number one!" he rises and yells, "What's wrong with being number two?" The students look at him. They stop chanting. He sits down, smiling and triumphant. (Albom, 1997, p.159)

We don't have to be number one at anything to live a meaningful and valuable life.

We can love again

My wife Mitzi, who is also a widow said, "You can love and be loved. You are loved and capable of loving."

I've found this to be true, even after a devastating event in our lives, like a spouse dying, we can pick up and love again because we are always worthy of love. Love renews when we choose it to, and since love is at the core of a meaningful life, our lives can have purpose and meaning again.

Chapter 7

Lessons from Morrie

Mitch Albom's *Tuesdays with Morrie* (1997) is full of profound wisdom and insights. As Morrie is slowly dying, he shares his insights with his past student, Mitch.

I read this book ten years ago and thought it was interesting and impactful, but not life-changing. Then I read it again recently. The difference between the first read and this one being that I had experienced Tiffany's death. It meant so much more this time. I realized how profound Morrie's insights are, and how much of a positive impact these ideas have when we see life from the perspective he shares.

Morrie's perspectives apply to Live Slowly as he talks about the importance of love. He explains why so many people feel like their lives lack meaning and gives insights into how we miss so much goodness in life by moving too quickly and searching in places we won't find happiness.

Here are direct quotes from the book. These ideas and insights stand out to me. I think you will appreciate them, too. To get the full impact of Morrie's message, I also encourage you to read the whole book.

"Love wins. Love always wins." (p. 40)

"He took more time eating and looking at nature and wasted no time in front of TV sitcoms or 'Movies of the Week.' He had created a cocoon of human activities— conversation, interaction, affection— and it filled his life like an overflowing soup bowl." (p. 43)

"So many people walk around with a meaningless life. They seem half-asleep, even when they're busy doing things they think are important. This is because they're chasing the wrong things. The way you get meaning into your life is to devote yourself to loving others, devote yourself to your community around you, and devote yourself to creating something that gives you purpose and meaning." (p. 43)

"The most important thing in life is to learn how to give out love, and to let it come in." (p. 52)

"Most of us all walk around as if we're sleepwalking. We really don't experience the world fully, because we're half-asleep, doing things we automatically think we have to do." (p. 83)

"Don't cling to things, because everything is impermanent." (p. 103)

"You can't substitute material things for love or for gentleness or for tenderness or for a sense of comradeship." (p. 125)

"'There's a big confusion in this country over what we want versus what we need,' Morrie said. 'You need food, you want a chocolate sundae. You have to be honest with yourself. You don't need the latest sports car, you don't need the biggest house. The truth is, you don't get satisfaction from those things. You know what really gives you satisfaction?' What? 'Offering others what you have to give.'" (p. 126)

"Do the kinds of things that come from the heart. When you do, you won't be dissatisfied, you won't be envious, you won't be longing for somebody else's things. On the contrary, you'll be overwhelmed with what comes back." (p. 128)

"'I believe in being fully present,' Morrie said. 'That means you should be with the person you're with. When I'm talking to you now, Mitch, I try to keep focused only on what is going on between us. I am not thinking about something we said last week. I am not thinking of what's coming up this Friday. I am not thinking about doing another Koppel show, or about what medications I'm taking. I am talking to you. I am thinking about you.'" (p. 135-6)

"Mitch, it was a most incredible feeling. The sensation of accepting what was happening, being at peace." (p. 172-3)

Chapter 8

Perceptions & Belief Systems

Less Effective Belief Systems Get Less Effective Results

The hardest part of making our lives better is that our belief systems get in the way. And changing our belief systems is a difficult thing to do. Almost everything we do is informed and influenced by our belief systems.

The trouble is that our belief systems are sometimes inaccurate, can be based on a single event that doesn't represent how things really work, and can be ineffective.

Having effective belief systems instead will improve your life.

A perfect example of an ineffective belief system is bloodletting. For about 2,000 years bloodletting was widely practiced as a way to cure and prevent disease. The practice came from a belief that the body is made up of four primary fluids that affect health and temperament. They believed that if there is an excess or deficiency in any of these fluids it affects health. If someone was sick, it was common for a physician to drain some of the blood from their body.

This belief was widely held until around the 1800's when modern medicine replaced it with a different belief systems. It is now known that bloodletting likely did more harm than good in most cases. This is an example of how a belief system informed behavior that was less effective. Modern medicine has a different belief system about how the body works, and it has a more effective way of keeping us healthy.

It's likely that at some future point our belief systems about cancer will change and will result in an improvement in the way we treat cancer.

When it comes to your life, the same principle applies. If you are stressed out, overwhelmed, or burned-out, it's because some of your belief systems are less effective. They are not wrong or bad, just less effective. Ineffective belief systems hold us back and keep us locked in to results we don't want.

One of my business partners, Del Walmsley, has been teaching people how to become financially independent since 1990. He retired when he was 32 years old by creating passive income streams—money that came in without him having a job.

He has helped several thousands of people retire early and live comfortably without financial stress. All together, he has taught over 30,000 people how to do this. Why have only about 10% actually done it? Because the others wouldn't or couldn't change their belief system about money. Del says his biggest challenge, the hardest thing he faces, is getting people to change their belief systems about money.

My grandmother emigrated from Russia when she was a teenager. She didn't know any English and had $10 when she arrived. Over time, she built a dry-cleaning business, purchased the building her business was in, and went on to buy houses and rent them out. She retired early and lived comfortably. Not wealthy, not poor—just comfortably secure. I don't know where she learned her belief systems about money, but she taught them to my mom.

My mom and dad followed the same path. My dad was able to retire from his private dental practice when he was in his 50's with the income they created from their real estate investments. They adopted a belief system about money and retirement that was effective.

Most middle-class Americans have a financial belief system of going to school, working hard for a company, putting money into a 401k, then retiring when they're in their 60's or 70's. Then they start spending their retirement money and hope they die before they run out of money.

Del's belief system, and the one passed down from my grandmother, is different. We believe in building passive income streams, reinvesting into more passive income streams, and retiring early. Your income streams provide for a comfortable life and you don't need to worry about running out of money before you die because your money keeps growing.

Even though it works and Del has taught thousands how to do it, most people just don't because they have a specific belief system that is difficult to change. It's very difficult to get people to change their belief systems about money.

As I wrote earlier, my oldest daughter has struggled with a difficult drug addiction. I have hope that she will overcome it and get her life back, but her belief system stands in her way. She believes that other people have caused her troubles. A more effective belief system is that her troubles are the result of her own choices. If she believes this, then she would be empowered. If her choices got her into the mess she's in, then her choices will also get her out.

An incident occurred recently that is an example of how a belief system affects the results we get.

I invited my daughter to live with me for eight months to help her get her feet on the ground. After about five months, I started dating Mitzi and spending more time in that relationship. My daughter felt that I was neglecting her and wasn't giving her enough attention. One weekend, she was visiting a friend in Prescott while I was in Gilbert, about 90 minutes away. I decided that after she had visited her friend I would drive up to Prescott, get a nice hotel, and spend one-on-one time with her that afternoon, evening, and the following day, giving her my undivided attention.

When I got to Prescott, she was very angry with me. Her belief system was that I had come to Prescott to interfere with her life and to control her. She refused to come visit me, and to this day is upset with me for being so controlling. Her belief system has led to difficulties between us. She is sensitive to being controlled, which is totally understandable given the awful things she has experienced in the drug culture.

What is sad is that her belief system leads to ineffective results. I'm unable to help her because she pushed me away. It breaks my heart, and I've felt much sadness over the fallout from that incident, and I know she has too.

A more effective belief system would be more positive and trusting. For example, "My dad listened to me when I expressed my feelings about not getting enough time and attention, so he came to Prescott because he cares. He was willing to put aside everything and do this for me, get a nice place to stay, and just tune in to me." If she had this belief system or could change it to something similar to this, she wouldn't have suffered so much with her negative feelings. She would have been more accepting of my help and could have made more progress in getting her life back.

We form our beliefs based on our experiences, our upbringing, things our parents and teachers have taught us, from friends, and from things other people do to us. For the most part, we don't question our belief systems or even recognize that we have them.

Belief systems about relationships, money, what is important and what isn't, what is a need or what is a want, and many other things inform your behavior and your choices every day. Your current belief systems are on autopilot. Observe them, become aware of them and then you can find that some are holding you back from getting better results in your life.

I invite you to become aware of your belief systems, learn which ones are limiting you, then search for more effective ones.

Adopting the Live Slowly principle is a new belief system. And it will get you better results in your life.

Many people believe that to be happy we need lots of money or a big house or a nice car or fame. Those are ineffective beliefs. A more effective belief is that to be happy we need to love and be loved, cultivate our relationships, and slow down. We need to simplify our lives, do less, and study what brings us joy and intentionally incorporate those things into our lives.

Be Happy Now

John Warrillow is a great business mentor who taught me how to systemize a business to work less and make more. In addition to writing a couple of books, he has a podcast where he interviews entrepreneurs who have created and sold their businesses.

In Episode 2 (2015), he interviewed Laura Coe. Along with her dad and brother, they grew Litholink to a $10MM business with 50 employees. In the interview, Laura explains how they sold it and shares some profound insights about life. Here's an excerpt:

> John: What's been the most surprising thing for you about selling a business? Is there something about life after selling your business that you could share for people to get ready for that experience themselves?
>
> Laura: The number one thing I say to everybody is that we as a country, as a culture, and particularly as entrepreneurs

hold our breath and we're going to be happy when. Like when I sell the company it's going to be this big moment and everything will just come together. The birds will sing louder, my whole life will be perfect, I'm going to have cash, I'm going to have this and that. I'll have arrived.

Selling a company is fantastic and having extra money is amazing and freedom is a beautiful thing, but it isn't a ticket for the rest of your life for happiness. I really highly recommend to everybody to enjoy the ride. To celebrate in every single solitary step of it. The process of building your first systems and getting your first clients, all of it should be celebrated. Waiting for that end goal is a big mistake.

Waiting for that end goal is a big mistake. What a profound insight.

Let's not wait to be happy. We can be happy now. If you aren't, then adopt the Live Slowly idea simplifier into your life. Live so life is peaceful and joyful now, not waiting for a big event to happen at some later date.

Changed Perspective of Consumption

One of the greatest fallacies in our culture is that consumption of goods and stuff is necessary and makes us happy. It's just not true.

In Benjamin Franklin's autobiography, he tells a story about when he visited a woman who lived in a simple room. All she had in there was a bed to sleep on, a simple table, a bowl, a plate, a cup, and utensils. She lived a simple life and was content. In that moment, he realized how little we actually need.

I'm not advocating we simplify to that level, necessarily. It would be hard for us to function in our society without any means of transportation or communication.

Michelle Steinke-Baumgard, author of *One Fit Widow*, wrote a great article called "Consume Life" (2017). She beautifully explains how the death of her husband of 15 years changed her perspective on a life of consumption.

The night after he died, as she sat in the now empty bed, she took a mental inventory of everything they owned. Two cars, a big house with a pool, beautiful furniture, and all the things they had from a life of consumption. None of that would bring him back. None of that would make her feel any better. She felt even lonelier in the midst of all that stuff.

I can relate. The morning after Tiffany died, I noticed her cell phone on her nightstand. Never to be used by her again. Never to call me or send another text message. Nothing she had, nothing we both owned, meant anything. That's why it was easy to give it all away. It was just stuff.

What I treasured were the quiet moments we shared. The trips we made. The talks we had. The life of consumption did nothing for me. The life of sharing love and time and life were what mattered.

Michelle had the same realization:

His death brought me full circle to his life.

A life that never cared about status symbols impressing the neighbors or living for job titles. The stuff we had accumulated was my idea, never his. In all honesty, I was the one buying into society's view of success and happiness. Turns out death teaches you the value and real meaning of life. Death teaches you that how society tells you to live is a set of rules you don't have to conform to or accept. Death teaches you that memories and experiences are real wealth for those of us who are left behind to make sense of life after loss. Death teaches you to live fully, bravely and honestly without the consumption of stuff as a means of artificial happiness.

The stuff you buy won't ever quench your thirst for happiness or meaning in this life.

Consumption is a trap of instant gratification and temporary stimulus.

The feeling of satisfaction quickly fades and must be replaced with more material objects, bigger, better and more elusive. Suddenly your life mirrors that of a hamster on its wheel. You run as fast as you can in the same direction, never getting anywhere new or worth going.

You are going to die.

The people you love are going to die.

That fact is unavoidable, and while unacceptable allow it to be a lesson for you now on your view of human consumption. You can make a choice to continue a life of stuff that won't sustain you on your darkest day or you can make a decision to skip the stuff and consume LIFE instead.

Perception Versus Reality

A challenge we all face is knowing the difference between what is actually reality and what is our perception of reality. It can be difficult to tell the difference. We automatically assume that what we perceive is reality. Then, we behave according to that perception.

The problem is that many times, our perception is not accurate. This can lead to ineffective decisions and trouble.

In a TEDEd video called "Rethinking Thinking," Trevor Maber (2012) explains how we think and how our thinking can lead us to incorrect perceptions. He explains that we process information sequentially in this order:

1. Take in raw data.
2. Filter the information based on our experience, preferences, and tendencies.
3. Assign meaning to the information and interpret what the information is telling us.

4. Develop assumptions based on the meaning we created in Step 3. This is where we start to blur the distinction between what is fact and what is story.

5. Develop conclusions based on assumptions. Our emotional reactions are created here.

6. Adjust our beliefs about the world around us.

7. Take action based on our adjusted beliefs.

He uses the example of pulling into a parking spot at a mall when someone cuts in front and takes the spot from us. Going through the steps outlined above, we assume that this person is rude and we have been wronged. We create a story about how that person thinks they are more important than everyone else. They are heartless. They need to be put in their place. We feel angry, frustrated, and vindictive. We may roll down our window ready to yell at the driver.

Imagine that he then walks over quickly and apologizes. His wife, who is due with their first baby, called from the mall and said she needs to get to the hospital immediately. Suddenly, our perspective changes and we re-adjust our reaction, wishing him well and encouraging him to move along.

This reminds me of a story Stephen Covey shares in *The 7 Habits of Highly Effective People* (1989). A man and his young children are on the subway in New York. The children are running around misbehaving and disturbing everyone. The dad does nothing, doesn't even seem to notice or care. When someone finally asks him to keep his kids in check, he apologizes and says they have just been to the hospital where his wife (the kid's mom) died.

We frequently and often come to incorrect beliefs through this automatic process of thinking and assuming. I'm not sure we can stop doing that. The important point here is to be aware that we do it and not hang on too tightly to the conclusions you make which are based on your perceptions and assumptions.

Communication researcher Sean Tiffee (2016) makes a strong case that there is a gap between perception and reality. He tells a very short story and asks us to visualize it. Here's the story: "Bob went to the beach to play fetch with his dog."

What kind of dog did you picture? Most people picture their own dog, or if not that, then either a Labrador Retriever or a Golden Retriever. But, whatever you pictured in your head was made up. What was the actual dog in the story? A cross between a Wolf and a Chihuahua, known as a Wolfhuahua.

We do this all the time. What the person talking is communicating is not necessarily what the listener is hearing. It's just the way it is.

Sean explains that there will always be a gap between perception and reality. Instead of ignoring the gap, he suggests that we mind the gap. Meaning, understand it's there and embrace it. The power in embracing this gap is that we have more empathy for other people because when we understand that we see things differently than other people, and their perceptions are just as valid as ours, then we can understand others.

We don't need to get mad, offended, or judgmental. Living is way more peaceful this way.

Isaac Lidsky is an inspiration to many people. He lost his eyesight over the course of a decade, starting at age 12. In spite of this, he managed to star in a sitcom at age 13, is the only blind person to have clerked for Supreme Court justices (he clerked for two of them), graduated from Harvard at age 19 with an honors degree in math, and is the CEO of a construction company.

In a talk called "What Reality Are You Creating For Yourself?" (2016), he explains that what we choose to see is our reality.

As a blind man, he confronts the assumptions other people have about his sight. He says that going blind taught him to live his life with his eyes wide open. He learned that what we see is not universal truth or objective reality.

What we see is unique and personal and is masterfully constructed by our brain. It is based on our understanding of the world, knowledge, memories, opinions, emotions, and mental attention.

What you see impacts how you see, and what you feel impacts what you see. He uses an example based on research. If you are asked to estimate the walking speed of a man in a video, your answer will actually be different if you are told to think about Cheetahs or Turtles while answering this question.

This may feel a bit unsettling to realize our perceptions are not necessarily linked to reality. However, it's a great thing. It means we have the freedom and power to decide how we see things, and how we see things determines what we can accomplish.

Isaac chooses to see a vision of what he will do that is not limited by his physical blindness. That is how he isn't confined to limiting belief systems.

Author Barrie Davenport wrote an article called "6 Steps To Untangle Reality And Perception" (n.d.). In it, she shares a story that illustrates how we perceive things differently and how our perception can often get confused with reality.

> Perception is the lens through which we view reality: ourselves, others and the world around us. However, the lens often gets confused with what is being viewed through it.
>
> To use a personal example, on a flight back home from vacation in Alaska, the pilot announced that we were flying around a storm.
>
> He asked that everyone remain in their seat as much as possible, as there was significant turbulence. Neither meals nor drinks were served. Even the flight

attendants remained seated throughout most of the flight!

Personally, I didn't know an airplane could move the way ours did. I braced for the worst due to all the instability. But, what clued me in to the fact that my perceptions might not correspond to reality was a man sitting right behind me on the flight. He was fuming that the crew was not serving food or drinks despite these minor bumps. That eventually got me thinking.

It may come as a severe shock if you haven't given much thought to this subject before, but our precious, cast-in-stone, objective beliefs are often totally in contrast to any reality. Or, more accurately, they are our perception of reality, rather than reality itself.

To him, the flight crew was overreacting. I suspected he was a frequent flyer who had been on flights just as turbulent. In the end, we were all hungry and thirsty, but landed on time without incident.

The lens through which I viewed the seemingly extreme turbulence led me to believe we were in danger when we weren't. My distress on this flight wasn't only useless, but it also instilled a fear of flying thereafter. I became hypersensitive to any turbulence.

In thinking about your life, consider that the way you're looking at a problem, challenge or issue might be part of the problem itself…

There is value in understanding the natural gap between our perceptions and reality. It means that we can have more empathy for others—more understanding, more love, more compassion, less judgement. This brings more peace, happiness, and joy into our lives.

It means we can create a vision and remove limitations in our belief systems. We can change our life from one of desperation to one of contentment.

It means we don't need to be angry, offended, or hold grudges. Letting go of these things has an amazingly powerful effect in our lives.

Applying the Live Slowly idea simplifier in your life is a way of minding the gap between perception and reality and gaining all these benefits.

Steps to Live Slowly

There are just a few simple steps you can follow to apply the Live Slowly idea simplifier in your life.

First, understand what brings you joy. Do this by creating a heart list and, for each item on the list, ask yourself why that brings you joy, then ask why again and again, going deeper and deeper.

Second, each day intentionally incorporate something into your life that brings you joy.

Third, periodically evaluate your life with a focus on simplifying. Reduce or eliminate things that are less valuable to your joy, so you have more time and focus for the things that do bring you joy.

It's that simple.

Did You Like *Live Slowly?*

Before you go, I want to say "Thank you!" for purchasing this book.

I have a small favor to ask. Will you take a quick minute to leave a review for this book on Amazon? Your feedback will help me continue to write books that you and others will enjoy and benefit from. And if you loved it, please let me know! :-)

My hope is that reading this book has helped you see how to have more life, more joy, and more purpose. Applying the Live Slowly ideas in my life has helped me through the struggles of having a drug addicted child, a wife dying of cancer, and rebuilding a new life after she died. I believe it can help you with the challenges and struggles you face every day.

There is a Live Slowly web site with a surprising name: http://www.LiveSlowly.com :) You'll find more help and support there as you work on living slowly.

References

Albom, M. (1997). *Tuesdays with Morrie: An Old Man, a Young Man, and Life's Greatest Lesson* [Kindle edition]. New York, NY: Crown Archetype. Retrieved from Amazon.com.

Covey, S. R. (1989). *The 7 habits of highly effective people.* New York, NY: Free Press.

Davenport, B. (n.d.) 6 steps to untangle reality and perception. *Live Bold & Bloom.* Retrieved from https://liveboldandbloom.com/07/self-awareness-2/6-steps-to-untangle-reality-and-perception

Fried, A. (Director). (2015). Niki Nakayama [Documentary series episode]. In D. Gelb (Creator), *Chef's table.* Netflix.

Holland, J. R. (2013). Like a broken vessel. The Church of Jesus Christ of Latter-Day Saints general conference. Retrieved from https://www.lds.org/general-conference/2013/10/like-a-broken-vessel

Lidsky, I. (2016). What reality are you creating for yourself? [Video file]. *TED.* Retrieved from https://www.ted.com/talks/isaac_lidsky_what_reality_are_you_creating_for_yourself

Maber, T. (2012). Rethinking thinking [Video file]. *TEDEd.* Retrieved from https://ed.ted.com/lessons/rethinking-thinking-trevor-maber

McGinn, B. (Director). (2015). Ben Shewry [Documentary series episode]. In D. Gelb (Creator), *Chef's table*. Netflix.

Steinke-Baumgard, M. (2017). Consume life. *Huffpost*. Retrieved from https://www.huffingtonpost.com/entry/consume-life_us_587943c6e4b077a19d180d9a

Suh, C. (Director). (2016). Water [Documentary series episode]. In M. Pollan (Creator), *Cooked*. Netflix.

Tiffee, S. (2016). Mind the gap between perception and reality [Video file]. *TED*. Retrieved from https://www.youtube.com/watch?v=8BL9uRJpTqY&feature=youtu.be

Trimble, G. (n.d.). Why we shouldn't ask the same people to help at church and in callings all the time, *LDSLiving*. Retrieved from http://www.ldsliving.com/Why-We-Shouldn-t-Ask-the-Same-People-to-Help-at-Church-and-in-Callings-All-the-Time/s/85076

Warrillow, J. (2015). Learn the secret to negotiating a sale with a multi-billion dollar corporation. *Built to Sell Radio*. Podcast retrieved from http://www.builttosell.com/blog/

Webb, J. (2017). The most productive people think this more often: Charles Duhigg. *Across the Board*. Retrieved from https://blog.trello.com/charles-duhigg-productive-people-think-this-more-often

About Damon

Damon is the father of five, grandfather of one, and a widower who lost his teen sweetheart to cancer in 2015 after 27 years of marriage. He is now married to a wonderful widow Mitzi who also encourages him to live slowly. He is a programmer, entrepreneur, author, and simplifier.

He writes the series of *Live Slowly* books, which help people lead a more enriching, joyful, peaceful, and satisfying life. They are practical, focused, and short. They are simple, because simplicity is best!

Made in the USA
San Bernardino, CA
16 January 2018